Today is Today

Marquita Ricketts

BookLeaf Publishing

Presentation by *BookLeaf Publishing*

Web: www.bookleafpub.com

E-mail: info@bookleafpub.com

ISBN: 9789395756518

First edition 2022

DEDICATION

Dedication is due to God– here's to one out the gate and many more to come.

I further dedicate this book to:

The little girl in me, who still needed something to believe in.

In the most not so cringe manner-- Lukas, Nite Lite, and Mr. Seven...thank you for growing me and reminding me that, while change is inevitable, it is always in my favor.

Family and friends-- new and old-- as you all shared a piece in the puzzle that is, currently, me.

Anyone who is living in doubt– may you find some of what you need, in this book.

ACKNOWLEDGEMENT

Thank you to God for the morning I "'stumbled" upon the Instagram ad that led me to be fearless, know that I am capable, and believe in myself just a little bit more.

Thank you to any and all hands that touch this book from start to finish. And just as many thanks to those who decided my book deserved a spot in their collection, on their bookshelves (both physical and digital), and in their hearts.

Much love and light, to all.

PREFACE

"Today is Today" started as a thought, that later wanted to become a script-- it still may be but let's take things in stride, I don't like too much pressure. As an actual book-- the thought hadn't crossed my mind but I saw an opportunity. So may "Today is Today" be the stepping stone we all need, to write that script that may still be.

Lost Thoughts On a Page

Tangible thoughts and misconstrued words
Exchanging nouns with misplaced verbs
Don't consider myself a poet or a lyricist
Finding pleasure in rhyming that with this
Spilling phrases out on a page
Only way to free my thoughts from their cage
Mind and tongue struggle to meet halfway
Self-doubt lingers from not knowing how to say
Is it because there are too many words to utter
Or do I thank this, that, and the ether?
Contribution to words contrived through
transcribe
Anymore, it's the only way I feel alive

August

Interpolated in context
As I figure out my next steps
Forward brings me closer, yet I feel I fall back
even further– when I leap
Trepidation forever orbinting my eternal
sunshine
Taking notes, as my everything flows
Wondering…if this is more of a lazy or white
river, kind of flow
While my heart's content in the unknown, my
mind continues to inquire

Maybe Tomorrow

Who or what has my mind running at 87 knots?
Daily, up 'til 3, with my thoughts tangled in
motion
"Did I do good as a mother?"
"Why did that person stare the way they did?"
"Tomorrow-- I need to focus more on that-- less
on this
On paper, it sounds like a great thought
But my mind could never be bought
Been a while since I've felt more than okay
Where today and tomorrow weren't, "just
another day".
I try to break the monotony
But even I, tend to fail me
Feel so alone in this overcrowded space
Angst-- brought forth by the voices in this place
Just like the days, they all blend together

Bitter Morsel

Never was any type of drug addict
But sex and alcohol were my two facets
Mixing beer and liquor, boys got me there
quicker
Never crossed my mind I was using, as a filler
My laughs and smiles were always
genuine...right?
How was I to know I wasn't right within?
How misplaced and displaced I truly felt-- not
knowing where I fit
I could harp on who failed me and when
But now that I know the basis of a trigger
The battles I once fought, now seem so meager

First Strikes

Falling, upward spiral
Lust, love, and/or denial?
Left turn, one way
Right turn, "one day"
Good intentions from a troubled heart
Always finishing, before I can start
Pennies, dimes, quarters
Cost of heart, surrounded by brick and mortar
When will the pain go away
Daily, overnight stay
Consistencies, inconsistent
Life changes...in an instant

The Sublurbs

Endless quarrels left to fate
Time, a quarter til late
Miss Chances at Unspoken Words
Your moments and memories, turn to blurbs
Once upon a space
Things weren't so hit or miss
Let's call it, "past" when we don't want to think
about it.

Enigmatic Therapy

One, two, ruminate
Inhale, exhale, illuminate
I mediate, just to dream
Sleep, only to live
Visions of times that didn't last
Reality lingering in the past
Skepticism creating a subconscious prison
In, out, enigma
Near, far, silence (tbc...9 days later)
Lost in miles of forgotten thoughts and lost hope
World's end, at the mercy of a rope
Can distance be true circumstance?
Or a lackluster fallacy we tell ourselves?
To leave chances, where we fell
Countless tasks, all in purpose
Aside from love and good intent, what is left?
Exhale, inhale, end of session

Groundhog Day Continuum

So many thoughts, words never form
New life, never to be born
To what length is my sacrifice
Deafening echos, at unbearable heights
Places and sights I'll never see
My best, that may never be
Writing my own fate, not knowing
The many seeds I've been sowing
Is it too late to change course?
Let it be natural or take by force?
Try to live beyond the curse
Struggling with my happiness first
Some day soon, I'll reach my destination

Incomplex Translations

Goosebumps...permeate my skin
Chills fill me from within
Have I traveled down the right path?
Or still, experiencing past life's wrath?
Makeshift boxes of totality
Are all that surround me
Far too long, I've lived de la morte
The judge and the jury, in my own court
Whispers of solace, come only in my dreams
At least there, everything is as it seems
I locate different parts of me
Living true life, infinitely, in various galaxies
Nothing out of context but in full perspective
I've seemed to have lost my words...

Backwards Speculation

10

Unmeasured innocence in cognitive dissonance
Knowledge dies in the epiphanied mind
When all the answers are precisioned excuses
Created from an egotistical plane
Never to be debunked by another's rebuttal

Socially Distanced

Yesterday's attachments become tomorrow's
detachments
Incomplete desires
As we settle for admirers
Follow for follow, like for like
Throw a heart, for a biased "right"
Socially connected...
While morally disconnected
Tall tales, posted in a story
Immortality archived via "memories"
Filters for days
Hiding our ways
Blue and green screens
Nothing's ever as it seems

The Illusory Race

Standing in the wake of your mercy
I beckon, while you grant me
Unaware of what I've asked
Lost in turmoil, until I grasp
Wishing to backtrack
On the wheel I created
Walking at runner's pace, I've lost where I'm at
Unsure thoughts and memories
Are they mine, do they belong to me?
Wish to fast track
Can I dream what's to come?
A new reality, beyond where I'm from?
So many answers, to so few questions
Extensive tests, wrapped in lessons
Standing at your mercy...please remember me

Just So You Know

I know my words could help someone
My stories could possibly bring freedom
The only problem is, it's hard
It's mentally tiring, trying to put so much into a
cohesive thought
Attempting to relive various moments, to let
someone know they are not alone
It's a lot...it's taxing
More often than not, when the thoughts form
freely, I don't have pen in hand
Or it can't move fast enough to keep up with my
mind
So please bare with me, I'm trying my best to get
(y)our story out

Banter

Learning
Steady growing
Don't take things personal
Or overthink to the ends of the world...
Words at a standstill

Brown Noise

15

My mind, sometimes riddled with theories
Words scattered about, loosely
Inexplicably escaping from my lips before I can
trap them
I found that, in quieting my thoughts…my
words lessened
Not because I had less to say but because I made
room to listen

Human Moments

My thoughts create books
Some Fiction, others Non-Fiction
On occasion, they create a genre of their own
While this may sound amazing to experience
This act creates chaos...often turning Fantasy
into Horror
Books that even Richard Tyler couldn't grow to
love
This is my darkness, this is my shadow

Deal, Your Way

17

The reality of it all is...
I'm trying to work on me
Inside and out
While trying to learn how to navigate my
relationships
And figure out what I like
While setting boundaries in those things that I
don't
All while keeping my inner child at bay but
With my company, instead of silencing her
altogether
…Is that a lot?

2314

By taking the long way
I felt like I was going the wrong way
Weaving in and out of consciousness
I just wanted to wake up and be home already

Fleeting

As pen hits paper
My thoughts begin to taper
Focus...focus
Do I write "just because"?
Or go where my mind travels?
...I begin to unravel
Ink leaking, trail of inner dealings
Heart's truer feelings
Guided by peace and clarity
I feel a nostalgic familiarity
The child in me comes out to play...
Spewing things the adult in me never could
Doing what I wish I should
Yearning to be out more frequently
Only I, can set me free

Coexisting with Choices

Dark space
Private corners
Lackluster scenery
Numbers doubling in triplets
That's how many times I've watched the clock
go round in this place I call my mind

NOW

In the moment's time I turned my phone off and back on. The "missed" notifications came pouring in– I then realized that the world does go on. It had managed to go on as it does, while I sat with my past.

As I sat with who was and who is. Familiar yet unfamiliar people, places, and things rolled before me on the old cassette. As I watched in slight confusion.

Uplayed narrative: "where did the time go...so much has changed...I wonder what happened to that person". Just as quickly as the tape ended, so did my sense of wonderment, of what was and what could have been.

www.ingramcontent.com/pod-product-compliance
Lightning Source LLC
Chambersburg PA
CBHW061328140726
47998CB00007B/2600